memories

Mama Knows Best

KATHRYN ANDREWS FINCHER

HARVEST HOUSE PUBLISHERS

EUGENE, OREGON

Acknowledgments

A huge "thank you" to:

. . . my wonderful husband, Jef, for loving me as a wife and mama.
And especially for being the greatest dad in the world.

. . . the greatest artwork ever . . . our beautiful daughters, Maggie and Kelley.
You are perfect models and model children. You are the light of our lives.

. . . my mama for her love and encouragement. I admire your strength and determination
as you continue to paint and "live" in spite of Parkinson's disease.

. . . my mother-in-law, Meryle, for sharing your knowledge from many years of working with children,
and for guiding me in the art of becoming a mama.

. . . the beautiful children in my paintings. Remember that your mama knows best. (And dad too!)

. . . my friends at DEMDACO for the opportunity to create and write the "Mama Says . . ." line of sculptures.
I pray that this line will encourage "Mamas" as they help their children to grow in wisdom.

. . . above all, my heavenly Father, who has entrusted me with the gift of art and joy of being a "Mama."

Mama Knows Best
Copyright © 2005 Kathryn Andrews Fincher
Published by Harvest House Publishers
Eugene, Oregon 97402

ISBN-10: 0-7369-1622-9
ISBN-13: 978-0-7369-1622-6

All works of art in this book are copyrighted by Kathryn Andrews Fincher and may not be reproduced without the artist's permission. For information regarding art prints featured in this book, please contact: www.kathrynandrewsfincher.com

Design and production by Koechel Peterson & Associates, Minneapolis, Minnesota

Harvest House Publishers has made every effort to trace the ownership of all poems and quotes. In the event of a question arising from the use of a poem or quote, we regret any error made and will be pleased to make the necessary correction in future editions of this book.

Scripture quotations are taken from the HOLY BIBLE, NEW INTERNATIONAL VERSION®. NIV®. Copyright © 1973, 1978, 1984 by the International Bible Society. Used by permission of Zondervan. All rights reserved, and from the King James Version of the Bible.

Printed in Hong Kong

05 06 07 08 09 10 11 12 / NG / 10 9 8 7 6 5 4 3 2 1

This book is dedicated to mothers who treasure the sounds
of tiny voices calling "Mama!" I am convinced that these endearing children
stretch a mama's heart so that it never returns to the same size.

Who Is Mama?

Behind every image is a message shared by the countless mamas, grandmamas, aunts, and other women who have shaped our lives. From generation to generation, they have loved us and taught us that the very ordinary things of living—tea parties and rain showers, playtime and chores—have a deeper spiritual meaning. Mama is the one whose guiding voice we hear, whose gentle touch we feel no matter how time and distance separate us. The thread of her wisdom is woven into the tapestry of our lives. Like a valentine that never fades, Mama's love is stamped on our hearts.

KATHY FINCHER

Mama's order was heavenly. It had to do with thoroughness . . .

and taking plenty of time. It had to do with taking plenty of time with me.

SUSANNAH LESSARD

Freckles Are Angel Kisses

Mama smiles, for freckles are not
imperfections but are as beautiful as spots
of color on a butterfly. Just like the
building of a cocoon, Mama wraps layers
of reassuring love around her daughter,
so that uncertainty will fly away and
inner beauty will take wing.

People are like stained-glass windows. They sparkle and shine

when the sun is out, but when the darkness sets in,

their true beauty is revealed only if there is a light from within.

ELIZABETH KUBLER-ROSS

4

A face
without freckles
is like a night
without stars.
AUTHOR UNKNOWN

Do Your Chores

Chores are not punishment;
they're good for you!
Mama knows that a bucketful
of chores today prepares a responsible
caretaker for tomorrow.

Demand the best from yourself,

because others will demand the best from you . . .

Successful people don't simply give a project hard work.

They give it their best work.

WIN BORDEN

Few things help an individual more than to place responsibility upon him, and to let him know that you trust him.

BOOKER T. WASHINGTON

You're a Bare Wonder!

Mama is in awe of the wonder
of her God-given child.

Ten fingers, ten toes
She's laughter and teardrops
So small and brand-new
And amazingly angelic
She's sent to bless you
She's one special baby
The best of life's treasures
And will grant and bless you
Many hours of great pleasure

AUTHOR UNKNOWN

A baby is . . .
a rose with all its sweetest
leaves yet folded.

LORD BYRON

Babies
are fresh from
heaven.

KATHY FINCHER

Always, Always Say Grace

*M*ama always, always prays.
She's grateful, too, because it's through God's
grace that her family is blessed.

Gratitude unlocks the fullness of life.

It turns what we have into enough, and more.

It turns denial into acceptance,

chaos to order, confusion to clarity.

It can turn a meal into a feast, a house into a home,

a stranger into a friend. Gratitude makes sense

of our past, brings peace for today,

and creates a vision for tomorrow.

MELODY BEATTIE

God has been gracious to me
and I have all I need.
THE BOOK OF GENESIS

God Has a Plan for You

Though Mama loves her child through and through,
she knows that God's love is even greater, and she yields
her little one to the Creator's perfect plan.

Whenever I held my newborn baby in my arms,

I used to think that what I said and did to him could have

an influence not only on him but on all whom he met,

not only for a day or a month or a year, but for all eternity—a very

challenging and exciting thought for a mother.

Rose Kennedy

God never puts
any person
in a space too small
to grow in.
AUTHOR UNKNOWN

Discover Your Gifts

$\mathcal{M}$ama knows that God promises spiritual gifts to all His children. Mama prays that her child will draw on these talents and gifts and use them to God's glory.

Big and Little Things

I cannot do the big things
    That I should like to do,
To make the earth forever fair,
    The sky forever blue.
But I can do the small things
    That help to make it sweet;
Tho' clouds arise and fill the skies,
    And tempests beat.

ALFRED H. MILES

Treat people as if they were

what they ought to be

and you help them to become

what they are capable of being.

JOHANN WOLFGANG VON GOETHE

Free the child's potential,
and you will transform
him into the world.

MARIA MONTESSORI

Take Care of Your Sister

ama is so glad that her younger
daughter loves to follow in the way of her
older sister. And she prays that no matter
how deep the sea of life, her daughters
will reach out for one another.

Sisters make the real conversations . . .

not the saying but the never needing to say is what counts.

MARGARET LEE RUNBECK

A sister is a gift from God,

sent from above to make life worthwhile here below.

AUTHOR UNKNOWN

My Little Sister

I have a little sister,
She is only two years old;
But to us at home, who love her,
She is worth her weight in gold.

We often play together;
And I begin to find,
That to make my sister happy,
I must be very kind.

I must not vex or tease her,
Nor very angry be
With the darling little sister
That God has given me.

AUTHOR UNKNOWN

Guard Your Treasures

*M*ama knows that children
will pick through, sort, and cherish
a barn full of so-called treasures.
She prays her children will hold tightly
and guard life's genuine treasures
that speak to the heart.

Have a heart that never hardens,

a temper that never tires, a touch that never hurts.

CHARLES DICKENS

Where your treasure is,
there your heart will be also.
THE BOOK OF MATTHEW

While our hearts are pure,
Our lives are happy
and our peace is sure.

WILLIAM WINTER

You Are My Treasure

$\mathcal{M}$ama is glad
when her children explore family
keepsakes. She knows that each child
is a treasure beyond price, a
precious gift from God.

Mama has a trunk full of treasures;

Hats, letters, photos of stuff she's done.

Mama hasn't the time for such treasures just now,

Because her "real" treasures are on the run!

KATHRYN ANDREWS FINCHER

I do not love him because he is good
But because he is my little child.

AUTHOR UNKNOWN

Here's the Church

*M*ama knows that the greatest gift
she can share is her faith. She prays that tiny
open hands will lead to big, open hearts.

*A little faith will bring
your soul to heaven;
a great faith will bring
heaven to your soul.*

CHARLES SPURGEON

Faith is an outward and
visible sign of an inward and spiritual grace.

THE BOOK OF COMMON PRAYER

Jesus Loves You

$\mathcal{M}$ama sings "Jesus Loves Me" as her
children follow with the motions. She rejoices that
His love will unite their family forever.

His love and His knowledge
are not distinct from
one another, nor from Him.
We could almost say
He sees because He loves, and
therefore loves although He sees.

C.S. LEWIS

God sees your problems
through your eyes
because He loves you.

CORRIE TEN BOOM

You're a Keeper

*M*ama rejoices that her young

anglers, as they cast their lines in life, are

docked securely in their family's care.

What greater thing is there for human souls

than to feel that they are joined for life—to be with each other

in silent unspeakable memories.

GEORGE ELIOT

A family is a place where principles are

hammered and honed on the anvil of everyday living.

CHUCK SWINDOLL

The family is a link to our past,
a bridge to our future.

ALEX HALEY

Mind Your Manners

*M*ama encourages climbing
and reaching for goals.
She cautions that it's not only
what you achieve, but also
how you achieve it that's important.

Manners are the happy way of doing things; each one a stroke

of genius or of love—now repeated and hardened into usage.

They form at last a rich varnish, with which the routine of life

is washed and its details adorned. If they are superficial, so are

the dewdrops which give such depth to the morning meadows.

RALPH WALDO EMERSON

If at first you don't succeed,
do it like your mother told you.

AUTHOR UNKNOWN

Share

*L*ike the rain's pitter-patter,
Mama repeats "Share, share, share."
For she knows that a sharing
nature will weather the storms of life
and help her children to shine.

Happiness is not so much in having as sharing.

We make a living by what we get, but we make a life by what we give.

NORMAN MACEWAN

Blessed are those who can give
without remembering, and take without forgetting.

PRINCESS ELIZABETH ASQUITH BIBESCO

To share often and much...
to know even one life
has breathed easier
because you have lived.
This is to have succeeded.

RALPH WALDO EMERSON

Take Care of Your Brother

Mama smiles. Her young angler
loves to follow in the wake of his older
brother. She prays that, no matter what
life may cast their way, her sons
will count on each other.

My brother and I would have preferred to start learning how to fish

by going out and catching a few, omitting entirely anything difficult

or technical in the way of preparation that would take away from the fun.

But it wasn't by way of fun that we were introduced to our father's art.

If our father had had his say, nobody who did not know how to fish

would be allowed to disgrace a fish by catching him.

NORMAN MACLEAN
A River Runs Through It

Let brother help brother.

PLATO

Eat Your Vegetables

$\mathcal{M}$ama teaches that good health
will enable her children to enjoy and
feast on the desserts of life.

The best six doctors anywhere,
And no one can deny it,
Are sunshine, water, rest, and air,
Exercise and diet.
These six will gladly you attend,
If only you are willing.
Your mind they'll ease,
Your will they'll mend,
And charge you not a shilling.

NURSERY RHYME

He who has health,
has hope; and he
who has hope,
has everything.

PROVERB

Love with All Your Might

"God, please give my child a strong
and caring heart." Mama knows that loving is easy.
It's letting go that's hard.

There never was any heart truly great and

generous, that was not also tender and compassionate.

ROBERT FROST

Many waters cannot quench love, neither can floods drown it.

THE SONG OF SOLOMON

I will hug
him, so that
not any storm
can come to him.

JULIAN HAWTHORNE

God Bless America

*M*ama says, "God bless America,"
and she means it with all her heart.
She prays that God will continue to hold
our nation in His hands and that
the hands of her children will be keepers
of the American dream.

We hold these truths to be self–evident,
that all men are created equal, that they
are endowed by their Creator with certain
unalienable Rights, that among these are Life,
Liberty and the pursuit of Happiness.

DECLARATION OF INDEPENDENCE

*The future belongs
to those who believe
in the beauty
of their dreams.*

ELEANOR ROOSEVELT

Don't Catch a Chill

Mama loves it when her daughter plays
little mama. She hopes playtime lovin' will grow into love
that endures any condition . . . like that of the dog.

There are persons so radiant, so genial, so kind,

so pleasure–bearing, that you instinctively feel in their presence

that they do you good, whose coming into a room is like

the bringing of a lamp there.

HENRY WARD BEECHER

The best portion of a good man's life is his little,

nameless, unremembered acts of kindness and of love.

WILLIAM WORDSWORTH

*Kindness is
the language which
the deaf can hear
and the blind can see.*
MARK TWAIN

Spread Your Wings

As each day flies by,
Mama lifts her son up in prayer.
For she knows that grounding
him in faith and God's Word will
empower him to soar.

Let us guide our children with wisdom.

Let us listen to their problems and help them find solutions.

Let us give them unconditional love—no matter what.

And when they are grown, let us find the courage to let go.

D. MORGAN

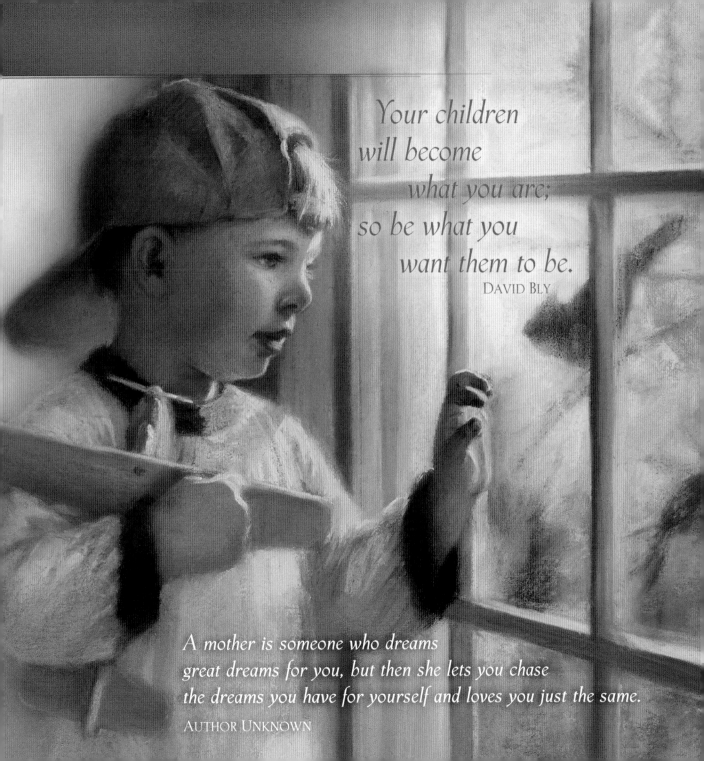

Your children
will become
what you are;
so be what you
want them to be.
DAVID BLY

A mother is someone who dreams
great dreams for you, but then she lets you chase
the dreams you have for yourself and loves you just the same.
AUTHOR UNKNOWN

Work Can Wait…

Mama knows God's creation
deserves attention. She prays both she
and her child will know to get out of
their shells and slow their pace, for it was the
turtle, not the hare, that won the race.

The mark of a successful man is one that has spent an entire day

on the bank of a river without feeling guilty about it.

AUTHOR UNKNOWN

There are many fine things which you mean to do some day,

under what you think will be more favorable circumstances.

But the only time that is yours is the present.

GRENVILLE KLEISER

44

Every now and then go away,
have a little relaxation,
for when you come back to your work
your judgment will be surer.

LEONARDO DA VINCI

You Are Precious in His Sight

Mama knows that
God's love for her and her children
is perfect. She prays that her
children will learn to reach out, embrace,
and return this precious love.

I felt the might and strength of God.

Sure was I of His efficiency to save what He had made;

convinced I grew that neither earth should perish,

nor one of the souls it treasured. I turned my prayer

to thanksgiving. The Source of Life was also

the Saviour of spirits.

CHARLOTTE BRONTË

Jane Eyre

46

Know that although in the eternal scheme of things you
are small, you are also unique and irreplaceable.

MARGARET LAURENCE

My mother was the making of me. She was so true
and so sure of me, I felt that I had someone
to live for—someone I must not disappoint. The memory
of my mother will always be a blessing to me.

THOMAS EDISON